LEO

ANTARES

EPISODE 5

9 th CINEBOOK
The 9th Art Publisher

Original title: Episode 5

Original edition: © Dargaud Paris, 2013 by LEO
www.dargaud.com
All rights reserved

English translation: © 2014 Cinebook Ltd

Translator: Jerome Saincantin
Lettering and text layout: Patrice Leppert
Printed in Spain by Just Colour Graphic

This edition first published in Great Britain in 2014 by
Cinebook Ltd
56 Beech Avenue
Canterbury, Kent
CT4 7TA
www.cinebook.com

A CIP catalogue record for this book
is available from the British Library

ISBN 978-1-84918-205-8

9th CINEBOOK
The 9th Art Publisher

'WE'D FINALLY ARRIVED AT THAT DAMNED PLANET FROM WHICH THE MYSTERIOUS BEAM THAT TOOK MY DAUGHTER ORIGINATED.'

'WE'D LEFT THE SPACESHIP IN GEOSTATIONARY ORBIT AND WERE NOW DESCENDING TO THE SURFACE IN THE SHUTTLE.'

'OUR DESTINATION: POINT X. THE SPOT WHERE OUR COMPUTERS PLACED THE ORIGIN OF THE BEAM.'

BAD LUCK – THERE'S A BIG STORM WAITING FOR US!

BRACE YOURSELVES. WE'RE IN FOR SOME SEVERE TURBULENCE!

EVERYONE, WE'RE NOW GOING TO MAXIMUM ALERT LEVEL! WE'RE LESS THAN 150 MILES FROM POINT X. IF THERE ARE ADVANCED EXTRATERRESTRIALS ON THIS PLANET, THEY MUST HAVE SPOTTED US A LONG TIME AGO.

MOST CERTAINLY THERE ARE ADVANCED EXTRATERRESTRIALS ON THIS PLANET! BUT I WILL TELL YOU AGAIN, FOR THE THOUSANDTH TIME: THEY ARE NOT A THREAT! THEY MIGHT EVEN SEND SHIPS TO ESCORT US TO A SAFE LANDING SPOT.

'THE INSUFFERABLE JEDEDIAH! I CHOSE NOT TO ANSWER HIM; TO IGNORE HIM RATHER THAN RISK LOSING IT.'

AN OBJECT JUST CAME INTO RADAR RANGE, PORT SIDE! D'YOU SEE IT, ALEXA?

YES, GOT IT. IT'S FAIRLY BIG – AND HEADING STRAIGHT FOR US!

ALEXA! COLLISION COURSE! WE MUST PULL UP!

DAMMIT! HANG ON TIGHT!

CALM DOWN! THEY'RE PROBABLY COMING TO WELCOME US! THEY'LL SLOW DOWN – YOU'LL SEE. YOU MUST HAVE FAITH IN GOD! IT WAS HE WHO LED US HERE!

LOOK OUT!

HOLY COW!

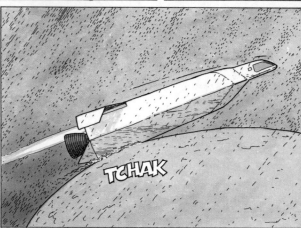

TCHAK

DID YOU SEE THAT?! SOME SORT OF AERIAL JELLYFISH!

PHEW! THAT WAS A CLOSE ONE! THAT THING MUST WEIGH TONNES!

IF WE'D TRUSTED IN YOUR GOD, MR JEDEDIAH, WE'D BE DEAD RIGHT NOW!...

2

4

'AFTER THAT FIRST ALERT, WE MANAGED TO LAND ON A SOLID ROCKY PLATEAU SOME 30 MILES FROM POINT X WITHOUT ANY FURTHER INCIDENTS.'

NO SIGNS OF ALIEN PRESENCE. NOT ONE RADAR AIMED AT US DURING OUR ENTIRE DESCENT. AND NOW THE SENSORS AREN'T DETECTING ANY KIND OF EMISSIONS FOR THOUSANDS OF MILES...

THAT'S STRANGE...

'ASTROPHYSICIST SURIA KHALEB WAS THE UN REPRESENTATIVE FOR OUR MISSION. I DIDN'T REALLY KNOW HER YET, BUT FROM THE START SHE'D STRUCK ME AS BEING A VERY SENSIBLE PERSON.'

HOW ARE WE GOING TO PROCEED NOW, COMMANDER KELLER?

WE'LL SEND A DRONE TO OVERFLY POINT X. BUT WE'LL HAVE TO WAIT FOR THE STORM TO ABATE FIRST. BESIDES, IT'S EVENING NOW. WE'LL WAIT UNTIL TOMORROW MORNING TO LAUNCH OUR CRAFT.

THIS IS ABSURD! WE HAVE ALREADY AGREED THAT THE PROBABILITY OF THOSE EXTRATERRESTRIALS BEING DANGEROUS IS EXTREMELY LOW. WE MUST THEREFORE APPROACH THEM WITH TRUST AND DIGNITY. SHOWING TOO MUCH DISTRUST TOWARDS THEM WOULD BE AN INSULT!

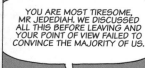

YOU ARE MOST TIRESOME, MR JEDEDIAH. WE DISCUSSED ALL THIS BEFORE LEAVING AND YOUR POINT OF VIEW FAILED TO CONVINCE THE MAJORITY OF US.

COMMANDER KELLER IS RIGHT, MR JEDEDIAH. YOUR INSISTENCE IS BECOMING A HINDRANCE AND COULD CAUSE POINTLESS TENSIONS AMONG OUR GROUP.

FINE. I'LL STOP TALKING!

③

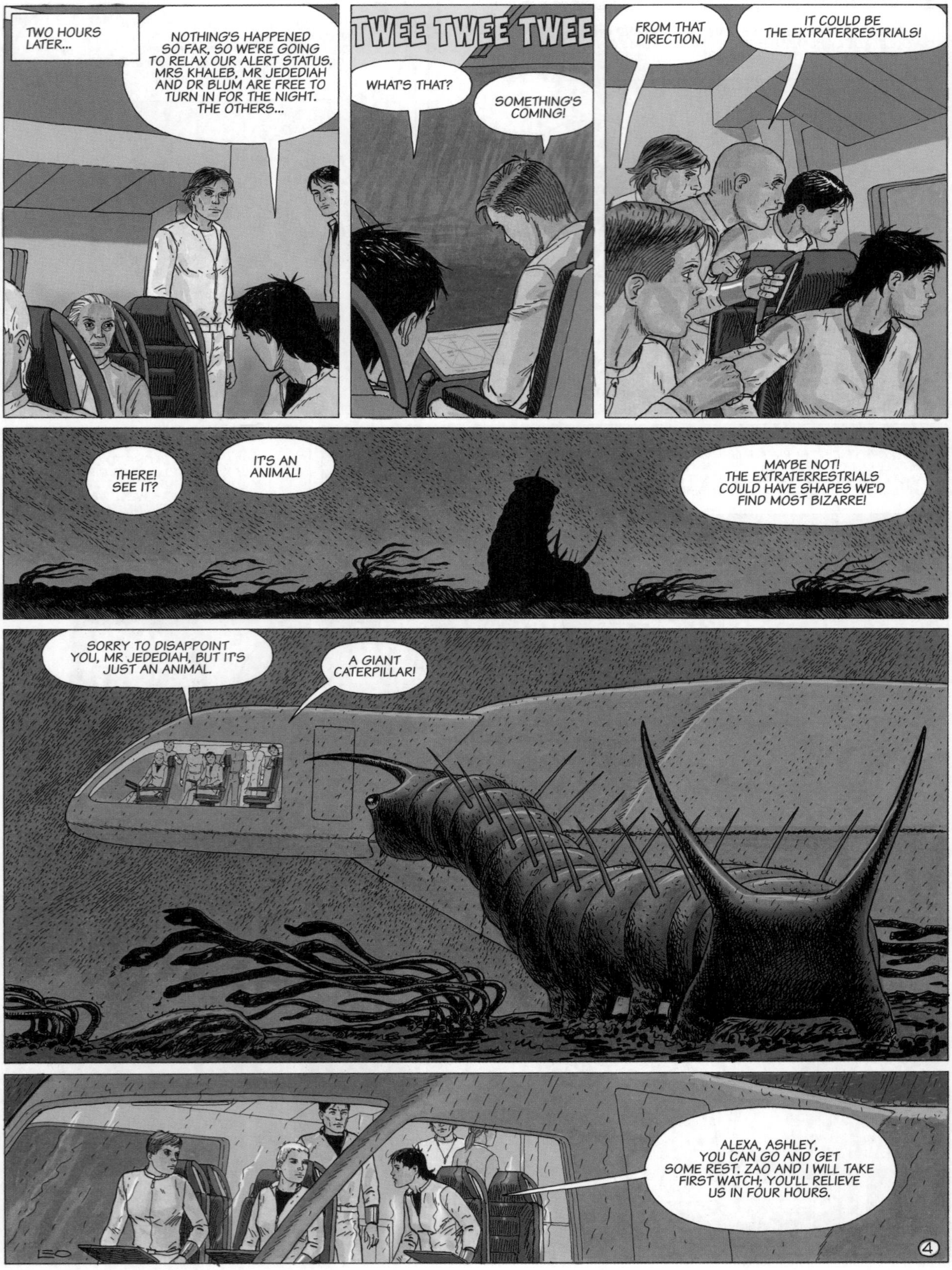
TWO HOURS LATER...
NOTHING'S HAPPENED SO FAR, SO WE'RE GOING TO RELAX OUR ALERT STATUS. MRS KHALEB, MR JEDEDIAH AND DR BLUM ARE FREE TO TURN IN FOR THE NIGHT. THE OTHERS...
TWEE TWEE TWEE
WHAT'S THAT?
SOMETHING'S COMING!
FROM THAT DIRECTION.
IT COULD BE THE EXTRATERRESTRIALS!
THERE! SEE IT?
IT'S AN ANIMAL!
MAYBE NOT! THE EXTRATERRESTRIALS COULD HAVE SHAPES WE'D FIND MOST BIZARRE!
SORRY TO DISAPPOINT YOU, MR JEDEDIAH, BUT IT'S JUST AN ANIMAL.
A GIANT CATERPILLAR!
ALEXA, ASHLEY, YOU CAN GO AND GET SOME REST. ZAO AND I WILL TAKE FIRST WATCH; YOU'LL RELIEVE US IN FOUR HOURS.
LEO
4

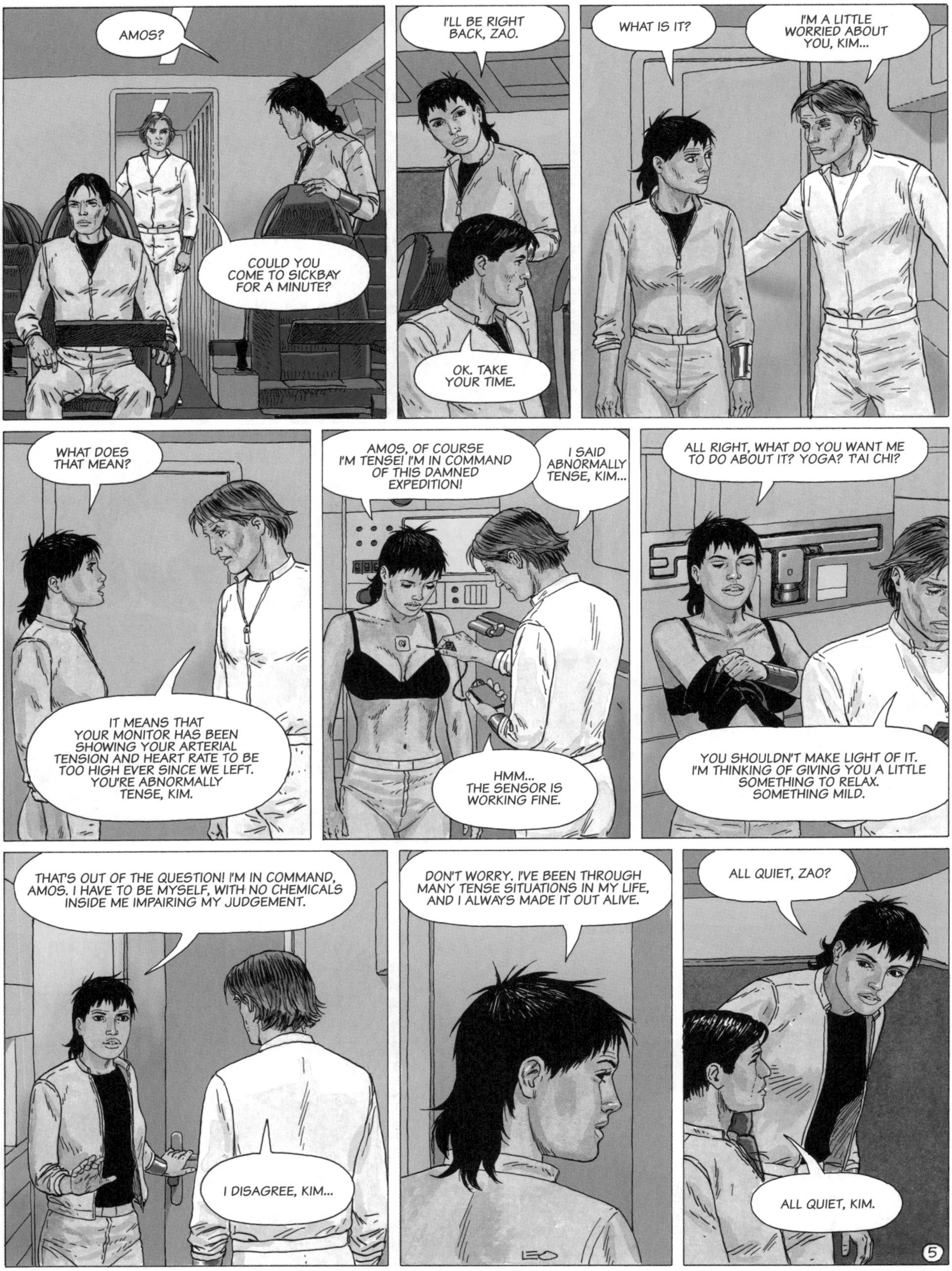
AMOS?
COULD YOU COME TO SICKBAY FOR A MINUTE?
I'LL BE RIGHT BACK, ZAO.
OK. TAKE YOUR TIME.
WHAT IS IT?
I'M A LITTLE WORRIED ABOUT YOU, KIM...
WHAT DOES THAT MEAN?
IT MEANS THAT YOUR MONITOR HAS BEEN SHOWING YOUR ARTERIAL TENSION AND HEART RATE TO BE TOO HIGH EVER SINCE WE LEFT. YOU'RE ABNORMALLY TENSE, KIM.
AMOS, OF COURSE I'M TENSE! I'M IN COMMAND OF THIS DAMNED EXPEDITION!
I SAID ABNORMALLY TENSE, KIM...
HMM... THE SENSOR IS WORKING FINE.
ALL RIGHT, WHAT DO YOU WANT ME TO DO ABOUT IT? YOGA? T'AI CHI?
YOU SHOULDN'T MAKE LIGHT OF IT. I'M THINKING OF GIVING YOU A LITTLE SOMETHING TO RELAX. SOMETHING MILD.
THAT'S OUT OF THE QUESTION! I'M IN COMMAND, AMOS. I HAVE TO BE MYSELF, WITH NO CHEMICALS INSIDE ME IMPAIRING MY JUDGEMENT.
I DISAGREE, KIM...
DON'T WORRY. I'VE BEEN THROUGH MANY TENSE SITUATIONS IN MY LIFE, AND I ALWAYS MADE IT OUT ALIVE.
ALL QUIET, ZAO?
ALL QUIET, KIM.
LEO
5

ZAO?

YES?

IT'S HARD TO IMAGINE THAT YOUR SISTER AND MY DAUGHTER COULD BE ALIVE SOMEWHERE ON THIS HOSTILE PLANET, ISN'T IT?

YOU MUST IMAGINE THEM TO BE IN A SAFE LOCATION, KIM. YOU MUST IMAGINE THAT THERE ARE UNDERGROUND INSTALLATIONS, CAMOUFLAGED BUILDINGS, SOMETHING LIKE THAT.

YES, OF COURSE. I'M BEING SILLY...

'NOTHING HAPPENED DURING MY WATCH WITH ZAO. AFTER BEING RELIEVED, I WAS SO EXHAUSTED THAT I HAD NO TROUBLE FALLING ASLEEP WITHOUT ANY CHEMICAL HELP.'

TWEEP TWEEP

YES?

YOU SHOULD COME DOWN TO THE HOLD. WE HAVE A PROBLEM.

WHAT IS IT?

THE DRONE...

WE CAME DOWN TO PREP IT AND FOUND IT LIKE THAT.

SOMEONE TOOK A HAMMER TO IT. THE ELECTRONIC GUIDANCE SYSTEM IS COMPLETELY DESTROYED – A TOTAL LOSS.

MR JEDEDIAH, COME DOWN TO THE CARGO HOLD IMMEDIATELY! I REPEAT, IMMEDIATELY!

YES?... YOU WOKE ME UP, YOU KNOW...

DID YOU DO THIS?

YES, OF COURSE. I COULDN'T ALLOW YOU TO RIDICULE US BEFORE THE EXTRATERRESTRIALS BY SENDING SOME PATHETIC DRONE TO SPY ON THEM! I DID IT TO SAVE OUR MISSION, SO WE COULD MAKE CONTACT WITH A SUPERIOR INTELLIGENCE!

OFFICERS SCOTT AND KOMAROVA, PLEASE ESCORT MR JEDEDIAH TO HIS CABIN AND LOCK HIM UP. HE WILL REMAIN UNDER ARREST UNTIL FURTHER NOTICE.

HEH HEH HEH!

DON'T BE RIDICULOUS! YOU DON'T HAVE THE AUTHORITY TO LOCK ME UP! I AM JEDEDIAH THORNTON, LITTLE LADY. I'M THE BRAIN BEHIND THE ANTARES PROJECT! I'LL NEVER LET A WOMAN LIKE YOU DICTATE MY BEHAVIOUR!

DON'T TOUCH ME!

KIM, NO!

COMMANDER KELLER!

PAF

YEAH!

YOU STRUCK MR JEDEDIAH!

DR BLUM, PLEASE EXAMINE MR JEDEDIAH, THEN TAKE HIM TO HIS CABIN.

HE SABOTAGED OUR DRONE, WHICH IS GOING TO MAKE OUR MISSION VASTLY MORE COMPLICATED, THEN DEFIED MY AUTHORITY.

BUT YOU STRUCK HIM! THAT'S UNACCEPTABLE!

I'M GOING TO HAVE TO REPORT THIS INCIDENT TO THE ADMIRAL, COMMANDER KELLER!

YOU MUST DO AS YOU SEE FIT, MADAM.

7

9

WELL, NOW WE HAVE NO CHOICE BUT TO USE THE HELICOPTER. LET'S PREP IT RIGHT AWAY. TWO-MAN CREW: ZAO AND ME.

ER... DON'T YOU THINK IT'D BE BETTER FOR ME TO GO WITH ZAO? YOU ALREADY HAVE...

NO, ALEXA! I SAID ZAO AND ME.

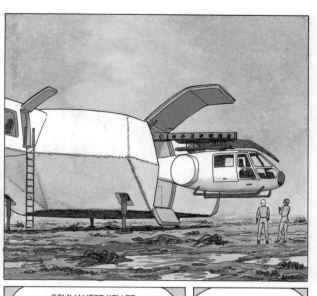

EVERYTHING'S READY. WE RAN THROUGH THE CHECKLIST AND THE ON-BOARD COMPUTER IS FULLY SET. YOU'RE READY TO GO.

VERY WELL. WE'RE UP, ZAO!

COMMANDER KELLER, I CONTACTED THE ADMIRAL ... AND HE SENT A MESSAGE TO THE CREW... AN IMPORTANT MESSAGE!

A MESSAGE... FINE. WE'LL LISTEN WHEN WE GET BACK.

I'M AFRAID THAT WOULDN'T BE RIGHT, COMMANDER. I MUST INSIST WE LISTEN TO THE MESSAGE NOW.

ALL RIGHT.

HELLO, ALL! I WAS TOLD ABOUT THE INCIDENT BETWEEN MR JEDEDIAH AND COMMANDER KELLER.

MR JEDEDIAH'S ACTIONS IN DESTROYING THE DRONE ARE EXTREMELY SERIOUS AND WILL HAVE TO BE SEVERELY PUNISHED. THEY COULD BE CONSIDERED MUTINY.

BUT IT WAS DECIDED THAT THE SANCTION WILL TAKE PLACE AFTER YOU RETURN, SO AS TO NOT ALTER THE CHARACTER OF YOUR MISSION. HE MUST NOT REMAIN LOCKED UP IN HIS CABIN. AT THE SAME TIME, COMMANDER KELLER'S ASSAULT AGAINST HIM IS ALSO A VERY SERIOUS OFFENCE.

IT SHOWS A LOSS OF CONTROL ON THE COMMANDER'S PART. WE ALL KNOW THAT SHE IS DEEPLY EMOTIONALLY INVOLVED IN A MISSION THAT, ACCORDING TO HER, WILL DETERMINE HER DAUGHTER'S FATE.

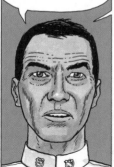

THERE ARE AGGRAVATING CIRCUMSTANCES DUE TO COMMANDER KELLER'S SERIOUS THREATS AGAINST MR JEDEDIAH, WHICH SHE MADE BEFORE MR ELIJAH THORNTON PRIOR TO THE MISSION'S DEPARTURE...

SUBSEQUENTLY, WE HAVE DEEMED THAT COMMANDER KELLER IS NO LONGER APT TO LEAD THIS MISSION IN AN EFFICIENT AND IMPARTIAL MANNER.

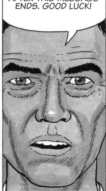

WE HAVE THEREFORE DECIDED THAT KIM KELLER WILL RELINQUISH COMMAND OF THE MISSION TO OFFICER ASHLEY SCOTT, EFFECTIVE IMMEDIATELY AFTER THIS MESSAGE ENDS. GOOD LUCK!

BUT...?! CAN HE DO THAT?! I MEAN, IS IT LEGAL?

YES, IT'S LEGAL. BUT COMMANDER KELLER CAN REFUSE TO OBEY IF SHE JUDGES THAT THE DECISION COULD JEOPARDISE THE MISSION.

I ACCEPT HIGH COMMAND'S DECISION. OFFICER SCOTT IS PERFECTLY QUALIFIED TO LEAD THE MISSION. YOU'RE IN CHARGE NOW, COMMANDER SCOTT.

AS FOR ME, KIM KELLER, KNOW THAT I WILL BE PRESSING CHARGES AGAINST YOU ONCE WE GET BACK.

ER... RIGHT. COMMANDER KELLER'S PREVIOUS ORDERS STILL STAND, THEN: OFFICERS ZAO AND KELLER, BEGIN YOUR RECONNAISSANCE OF POINT X RIGHT AWAY. WE'RE ALREADY WELL BEHIND SCHEDULE.

I WILL BE ON THIS SORTIE, TOO.

WHAT?!

IT'S WRITTEN IN THE MISSION PROTOCOL: I MUST TAKE PART IN ANY ACTIVITY THAT COULD LEAD TO AN ENCOUNTER WITH THE EXTRATERRESTRIALS.

HE'S RIGHT, COMMANDER SCOTT. IT'S WRITTEN IN THE PROTOCOL – AND WE ALL SIGNED IT...

GO AND GET READY, JEDEDIAH THORNTON. WE'RE ALREADY LATE.

YES... FINE, BUT OFFICER KELLER IS IN COMMAND OF THE SORTIE. IS THAT CLEAR?

I'M REALLY SORRY, KIM!

DON'T WORRY ABOUT IT, ASHLEY... MAYBE IT'S BETTER THIS WAY.

'WE FLEW OVER A ROCKY PLATEAU THAT, ACCORDING TO OUR MAP, WOULD CUT OFF ABRUPTLY ABOUT 13 MILES AHEAD AND GIVE WAY TO A PLAIN SOME 2,000 FEET BELOW.'

SLOW DOWN, ZAO. WE SHOULD BE ABLE TO SEE POINT X ONCE WE REACH THE PLATEAU'S EDGE.

SLOWLY NOW... STAY CLOSE TO THE GROUND.

'WHAT WERE WE GOING TO FIND AT POINT X? A FUTURISTIC EXTRATERRESTRIAL BASE? A MASSIVE ALIEN SHIP JUST LIKE IN TV SERIES? I WAS SO ANXIOUS I COULD FEEL MY HEART BEAT LOUDLY AGAINST MY CHEST.'

'BUT REACHING THE EDGE OF THE ROCKY PLATEAU ONLY BROUGHT DISAPPOINTMENT...'

THERE'S NOTHING!

⑩

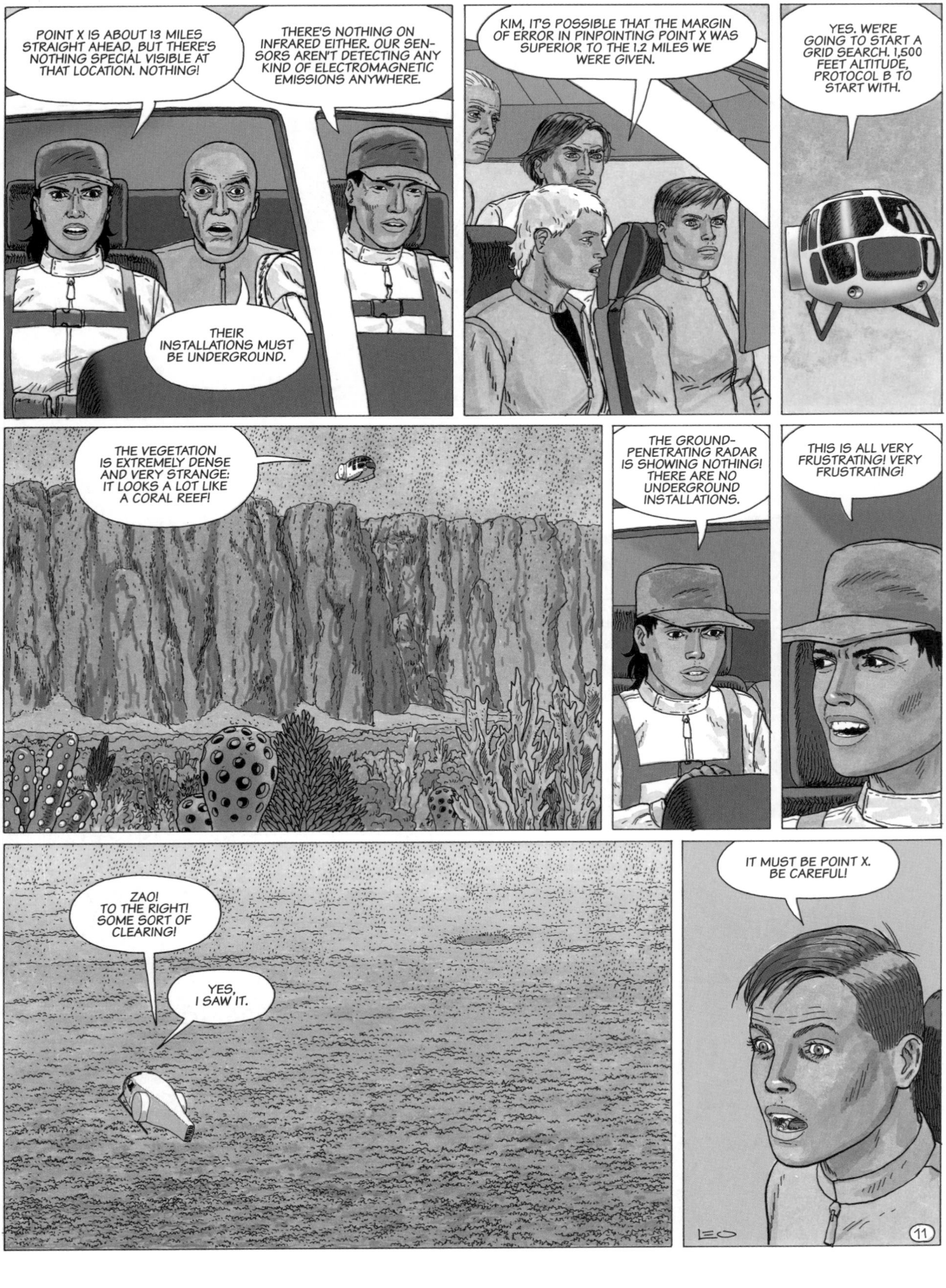
POINT X IS ABOUT 13 MILES STRAIGHT AHEAD, BUT THERE'S NOTHING SPECIAL VISIBLE AT THAT LOCATION. NOTHING!
THERE'S NOTHING ON INFRARED EITHER. OUR SENSORS AREN'T DETECTING ANY KIND OF ELECTROMAGNETIC EMISSIONS ANYWHERE.
THEIR INSTALLATIONS MUST BE UNDERGROUND.
KIM, IT'S POSSIBLE THAT THE MARGIN OF ERROR IN PINPOINTING POINT X WAS SUPERIOR TO THE 1.2 MILES WE WERE GIVEN.
YES. WE'RE GOING TO START A GRID SEARCH. 1,500 FEET ALTITUDE, PROTOCOL B TO START WITH.
THE VEGETATION IS EXTREMELY DENSE AND VERY STRANGE: IT LOOKS A LOT LIKE A CORAL REEF!
THE GROUND-PENETRATING RADAR IS SHOWING NOTHING! THERE ARE NO UNDERGROUND INSTALLATIONS.
THIS IS ALL VERY FRUSTRATING! VERY FRUSTRATING!
ZAO! TO THE RIGHT! SOME SORT OF CLEARING!
YES, I SAW IT.
IT MUST BE POINT X. BE CAREFUL!
LEO
11

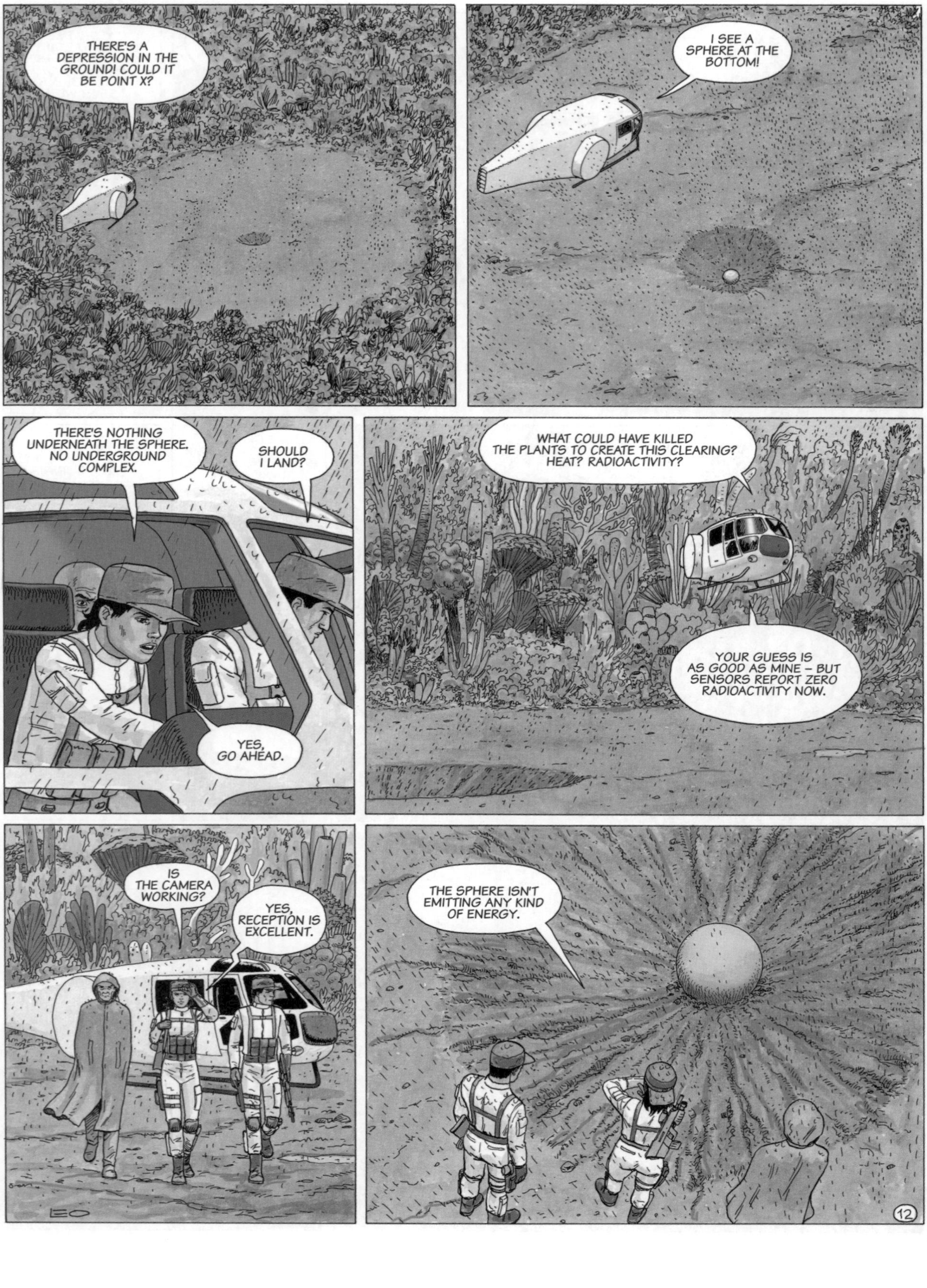
THERE'S A DEPRESSION IN THE GROUND! COULD IT BE POINT X?
I SEE A SPHERE AT THE BOTTOM!
THERE'S NOTHING UNDERNEATH THE SPHERE. NO UNDERGROUND COMPLEX.
SHOULD I LAND?
YES, GO AHEAD.
WHAT COULD HAVE KILLED THE PLANTS TO CREATE THIS CLEARING? HEAT? RADIOACTIVITY?
YOUR GUESS IS AS GOOD AS MINE – BUT SENSORS REPORT ZERO RADIOACTIVITY NOW.
IS THE CAMERA WORKING?
YES, RECEPTION IS EXCELLENT.
THE SPHERE ISN'T EMITTING ANY KIND OF ENERGY.
LEO
12

KEEP YOUR EYES PEELED, ZAO. THE JUNGLE AROUND US SEEMS HIGHLY DANGEROUS.

FIRST WEIRD THING TO REPORT: WITH ALL THE RAIN FALLING AROUND HERE, THIS HOLE SHOULD BE FILLED WITH WATER!

THE SPHERE IS PERFECTLY SMOOTH AND CLEAN. UNNATURALLY CLEAN FOR SOMETHING EXPOSED TO THE WEATHER.

TOUCHING IT, IT FEELS LIKE CERAMIC, DOESN'T CONDUCT HEAT, AND SEEMS TO BE EXTREMELY COMPACT AND HEAVY. I'M GOING TO...

WHAT IS IT, KIM?

IT'S STICKY! LIKE WHEN YOU TOUCH A VERY COLD SURFACE. EXCEPT IT'S NOT COLD.

HOW DOES THAT WORK?

NO IDEA, KIM. WE HAVE TO DO AN IN-DEPTH EXAMINATION OF THAT SPHERE. X-RAY IT, FOR STARTERS.

BUT TO DO THAT, YOU'LL HAVE TO BRING IT BACK HERE. WE HAVE A FIVE-TONNE HOIST. THAT SHOULD BE ENOUGH – I'M SENDING IT TO YOU.

BAFFLING, ISN'T IT? I WAS CONVINCED WE WERE GOING TO FIND SOMETHING ENORMOUS AND HIGHLY COMPLEX AT THIS POINT X. BECAUSE SENDING AN ENERGY BEAM TO A PLANET SEVERAL MILLION MILES AWAY WOULD REQUIRE A DEVICE A DAMN SIGHT BIGGER THAN THIS SPHERE!

IT'S BAFFLING, ALL RIGHT...

GOD DID NOT LEAD US HERE SIMPLY SO WE COULD FIND A SIMPLE SPHERE. YOU ARE DEMONSTRATING PESSIMISM TYPICAL OF UNBELIEVERS!

13

SPARE US YOUR PIOUS CERTAINTIES, JEDEDIAH THORNTON...

WATCH OUT! AN ANIMAL.

SHOOT IT?

LET'S WAIT AND SEE IF...

SLAPT

WOW! A GIANT CARNIVOROUS PLANT! UNLESS THIS ISN'T A PLANT BUT AN ANIMAL – AN UNMOVING ANIMAL CLINGING TO THE GROUND.

YES... THERE ARE THINGS LIKE THAT ON MY HOME PLANET, ALDEBARAN. AT ANY RATE, IT'S CLEAR PROOF THAT THIS JUNGLE IS EXTREMELY DANGEROUS!

SOON AFTER...

KIM, THE HOIST IS THERE.

YES, I SEE IT. YOU CAN TRANSFER CONTROL TO ME.

DONE. THE SURFACE IS VERY SMOOTH AND ALLOWS THE SUCTION PAD 100% FASTENING.

I'M STARTING TO LIFT...

BEEP OVERLOAD DETECTED. OPERATION CANCELLED.

ACCORDING TO THE HOIST'S SENSORS, THIS SPHERE WEIGHS OVER 200 TONNES!

OVER 200 TONNES? A SPHERE THAT SIZE?! OUR SHUTTLE IS LIGHTER THAN THAT!

COULD IT BE A SENSOR MALFUNCTION?

WELL, THERE'S NOTHING WE CAN DO FOR THE MOMENT. SEND THE HOIST HOME AND COME BACK. OUR INSTRUMENTS SHOW THAT A STORM IS COMING – A BIG ONE. YOU MUST GET BACK BEFORE IT ARRIVES!

THE SUCTION PAD IS STILL LOCKED ONTO THE SPHERE! UNBELIEVABLE!

WHAT THE BLAZES IS THIS THING?

THERE! YOU CAN RESUME CONTROL OF THE HOIST.

UNDER-STOOD.

ZZMMMMMMMMM

WHAT IS...?!

SHUTTLE, ARE YOU HEARING THIS? THE SPHERE IS EMITTING A VERY LOUD SOUND – SO LOUD THE GROUND IS SHAKING!

YES, WE'RE HEARING IT!

MMMMMM

THE SOUND IS GETTING LOUDER, AND SO IS THE VIBRATING! THE SPHERE HAS BECOME DARKER AND DULLER.

15

STEP AWAY FROM THE SPHERE!

HURRY, KIM, IT'S TOO RISKY!

MMMMM

LOOK!

IT'S MOVING! IT'S LIFTING OFF THE GROUND!

MMMMM

COME ON! LET'S GET BACK!

MMMMMMM

THE SOUND AND THE VIBRATIONS HAVE STOPPED. EVERYTHING'S BACK TO NORMAL – EXCEPT THAT THIS 200-TONNE SPHERE IS JUST FLOATING IN MID-AIR LIKE A BALLOON!

COME BACK! THE STORM'S GETTING CLOSE. WE'LL RETURN TO THE SITE LATER.

NO!

DON'T YOU UNDERSTAND?! THE SPHERE REACTED TO OUR PRESENCE. THAT MEANS THE EXTRATERRESTRIALS HAVE FINALLY NOTICED WE'RE HERE! THEY MUST BE ON THEIR WAY TO MEET US. WE HAVE TO STAY HERE AND WAIT FOR THEM!

YOU FORGET THE STORM, MR JEDEDIAH! IT WOULD KEEP YOU ON THE GROUND FOR WHO KNOWS HOW LONG! YOU CAN'T RISK SPENDING THE NIGHT IN THIS JUNGLE! YOU MUST COME BACK IMMEDIATELY!

NO! WE MUST STAY! WE WILL PRAY! GOD WILL PROTECT US! THE EXTRATERRESTRIALS WILL COME! THEY'LL PROTECT US!

YOU'RE RAVING, MR JEDEDIAH! COME BACK – THAT'S AN ORDER! KIM, ZAO, BRING HIM BACK BY FORCE IF YOU HAVE TO!

(16)

18

YOU HEARD HER, JEDEDIAH. CLIMB ABOARD OR I'LL TAKE GREAT PLEASURE IN KNOCKING YOU OUT...

LORD, OH LORD, WHY DO YOU KEEP ME FROM SERVING YOU PROPERLY BY SADDLING ME WITH PEOPLE OF SUCH POOR QUALITY?

PHEW! MIGHTY FRUSTRATING, ISN'T IT?

AT LEAST THERE'S THE FACT THAT THE SPHERE SEEMED TO REACT TO YOUR PRESENCE. THAT'S AN IMPORTANT FIRST STEP.

YES, BUT ALL THERE IS AT POINT X IS THAT LITTLE SPHERE – AND NOTHING ELSE! NO UNDERGROUND INSTALLATIONS. DON'T FORGET I CAME HERE TO LOOK FOR MY DAUGHTER! DO YOU THINK SHE'S THERE, INSIDE THAT DAMNED SPHERE?!

IT'S POSSIBLE THE SPHERE IS NO MORE THAN SOME SORT OF BEACON, KIM. SOMETHING TO GUIDE POSSIBLE ALIEN SPACE-SHIPS – WHICH WOULD BE THE ACTUAL SOURCE OF THE BEAM THAT TOOK YOUR DAUGHTER.

HMM... IN THAT CASE, JEDEDIAH MIGHT BE RIGHT: THE SPHERE ALERTED THE EXTRATERRESTRIALS TO OUR PRESENCE, AND THEY'LL COME BY TO SEE WHAT'S GOING ON. WE'LL HAVE TO BE THERE TO WAIT FOR THEM.

NOT NECESSARILY. OUR SHUTTLE IS RIGHT NEXT DOOR TO THE SPHERE – THE CRUDEST RADAR WOULD DETECT IT. IF THEY COME TO MEET US, THEY'LL KNOW WHERE TO FIND US.

ONCE THE STORM HAS PASSED, WE'LL GO BACK AND ESTABLISH AN OBSERVATION POST BY THE SPHERE...

...WHILE THE HELICOPTER WILL MAKE A WIDER SWEEP OF THE AREA TO MAKE SURE THE REAL POINT X ISN'T SIMPLY WALKING DISTANCE FROM THERE, COMPLETE WITH AN ENTRANCE TO A PROPER UNDERGROUND COMPLEX.

MAY I?

OF COURSE – COME IN!

TIRED?

TIRED AND ON THE EDGE OF A BREAKDOWN!

WHY IS THAT?

THIS PLANET IS A NIGHTMARE! I DON'T WANT TO THINK OF MY LITTLE LYNN BEING HERE! MY ONLY HOPE WAS THAT THERE MIGHT BE SOMETHING UNDERGROUND – BUT THERE'S NOTHING! ALL WE FOUND IS A SMALL CERAMIC SPHERE THAT CAN DO A FEW TRICKS! I FEEL LIKE CRYING, ALEXA!

YOU'RE OVERSIMPLIFYING, KIM. WITH ITS INSANE WEIGHT AND ITS ABILITY TO DEFY THE LAWS OF GRAVITY, THAT SPHERE IS UNDOUBTEDLY SEVERAL CENTURIES AHEAD OF US, TECHNOLOGICALLY SPEAKING! THAT'S A VITAL PIECE OF DATA.

AND THERE'S THE POSSIBILITY THAT THE EXTRATERRESTRIALS ARE THERE, SOMEWHERE, IN THEIR SPACESHIPS ... WHERE LYNN WOULD BE SAFE AND SOUND.

YES, MAYBE... BUT THAT'S PURE SPECULATION! YOU HAVE TO ADMIT IT'S ALL PRETTY HARD TO SWALLOW!

ALL RIGHT, I HAVE TO CALM DOWN... THEY WERE RIGHT TO REMOVE ME FROM COMMAND, ANYWAY. MY ONLY REGRET IS THAT THEY DIDN'T PUT YOU IN CHARGE INSTEAD OF ASHLEY.

ASHLEY'S QUALIFIED FOR THE JOB.

NO, SHE'S NOT. I SAW HER CRACK – SHE'S NOT TOUGH ENOUGH. SHE HIDES BEHIND THE FACADE OF AN EXPERIENCED OFFICER, BUT SHE'S NOT TOUGH ENOUGH.

I EVEN WONDER WHY I DIDN'T STRIKE HER FROM THE LIST OF MISSION PERSONNEL. I HAD THE POWER TO STOP HER FROM JOINING US, BUT I DIDN'T – I DIDN'T WANT TO HURT HER CAREER. WHAT AN IRRESPONSIBLE ARGUMENT!

OH, COME ON, STOP THAT!

I'M SO RELIEVED YOU'RE WITH ME! SO RELIEVED!

TRY TO GET SOME SLEEP. YOU LOOK TIRED. YOU NEED REST.

AMOS? WOULD YOU MIND COMING OVER?

WHAT IS IT? NOT FEELING WELL?

NO, I'M NOT FEELING WELL...

...I'M TERRIFIED FOR MY DAUGHTER, AMOS, AND I FEEL LIKE CRYING UNTIL I DIE! STAY WITH ME. SLEEP WITH ME.

I'D GIVE ANYTHING TO MAKE SURE THIS ENDS WELL, KIM...

I DON'T WANT THINGS BETWEEN US TO HAPPEN IN THIS WAY... YOU'RE IN TREMENDOUS EMOTIONAL DISTRESS AND...

I DON'T CARE, AMOS. I WANT IT...

MEANWHILE, A LONG WAY AWAY ON THE NEIGHBOURING PLANET, AT THE ANTARES PROJECT BASE CAMP...

WHOA! LORNA, I CAN HARDLY RECOGNISE YOU! YOU LOOK FANTASTIC!

YOU THINK I LOOK OK? THIS ISN'T TOO MUCH, IS IT?

DEPENDS WHERE YOU'RE GOING AND WHO YOU'RE MEETING...

I'M IN LOVE, MAI LAN! I FOUND THE MOST WONDERFUL PERSON IN THE WORLD! SOMEONE WHO UNDERSTANDS ME AND ACCEPTS ME AS I AM!

GREAT! WHO IS SHE? DO I KNOW HER?

LEO 19

21

NO, YOU DON'T KNOW HER. HERE, LET ME SHOW YOU...

THAT'S HER. HER NAME'S LANA.

SHE'S VERY PRETTY!

I WANTED TO ASK YOU A FAVOUR... SHE'S COMING HERE LATER... IF YOU COULD MAYBE GIVE US SOME TIME ALONE...

AH... I'M TIRED, LORNA. WORKING IN THE ORCHARDS IS HARD WORK, YOU KNOW... WHY DON'T YOU TWO GO OUT?

BECAUSE HER PARENTS ARE ALSO MEMBERS OF THAT DAMNED CULT, LIKE MINE. IF THEY EVER HEARD ABOUT US BEING TOGETHER, THEY'D KILL US!

OK, FINE... BUT TRY TO FIND ANOTHER WAY NEXT TIME, ALL RIGHT?

YOU'RE THE BEST, MAI LAN! IN EXCHANGE, I'LL CLEAN UP THE ROOM FOR A MONTH!

WOW! I MUST SAY I'D FANTASISED ABOUT THIS MOMENT, BUT REALITY WAS BEYOND MY WILDEST DREAMS!

YOU'RE CRYING...

AMOS...

HMM?

DON'T ASK ME ANY QUESTIONS ABOUT US – WHAT WE'VE JUST DONE AND ALL THAT. OK?

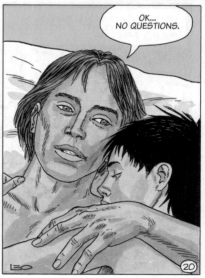

OK... NO QUESTIONS.

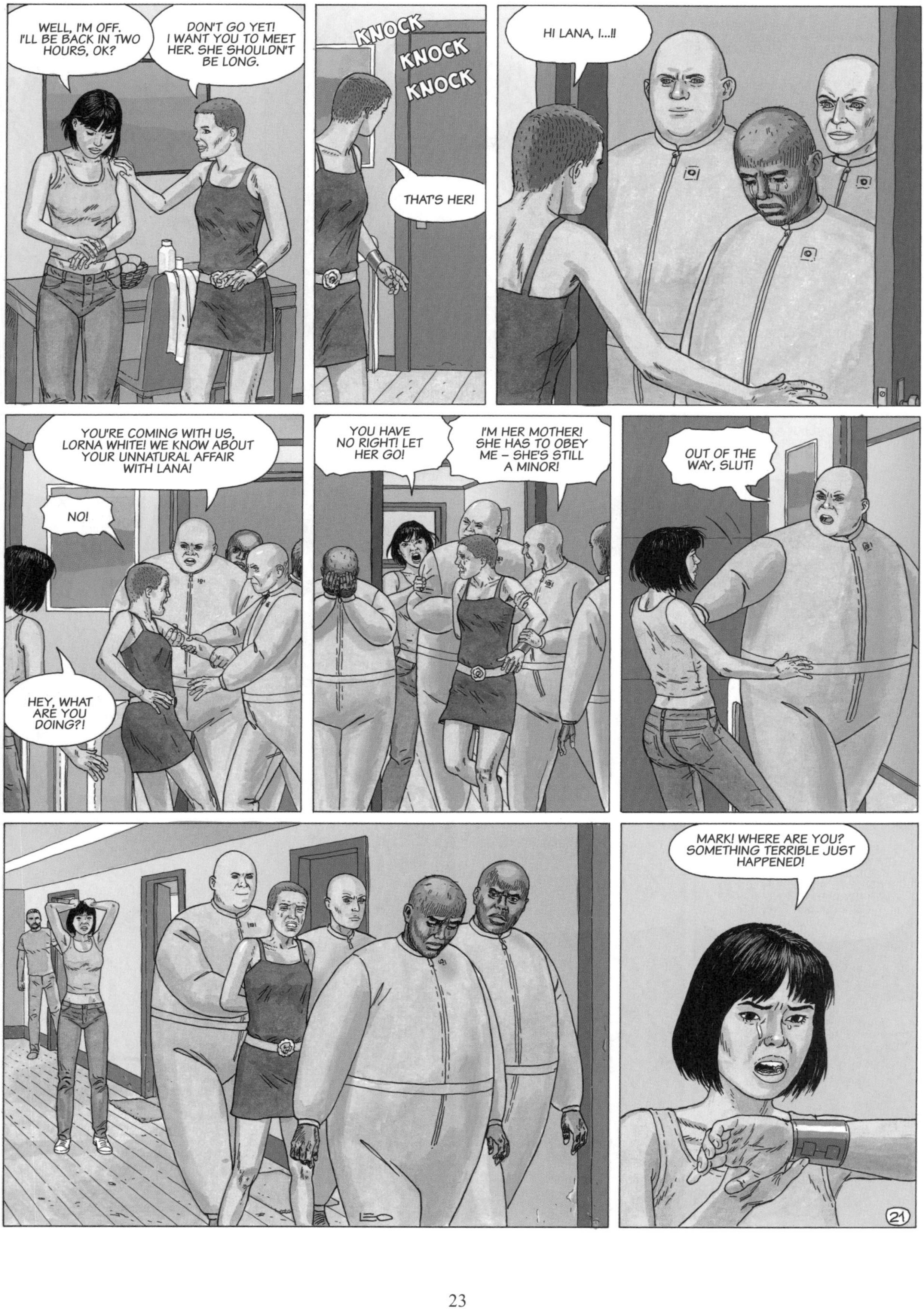
WELL, I'M OFF. I'LL BE BACK IN TWO HOURS, OK?
DON'T GO YET! I WANT YOU TO MEET HER. SHE SHOULDN'T BE LONG.
KNOCK
KNOCK
KNOCK
THAT'S HER!
HI LANA, I...!!
YOU'RE COMING WITH US, LORNA WHITE! WE KNOW ABOUT YOUR UNNATURAL AFFAIR WITH LANA!
NO!
HEY, WHAT ARE YOU DOING?!
YOU HAVE NO RIGHT! LET HER GO!
I'M HER MOTHER! SHE HAS TO OBEY ME – SHE'S STILL A MINOR!
OUT OF THE WAY, SLUT!
MARK! WHERE ARE YOU? SOMETHING TERRIBLE JUST HAPPENED!
LEO
21

THIS IS ASHLEY SCOTT. WE HAVE A PROBLEM. EVERYONE TO THE COCKPIT, PLEASE!

WHAT?!...

KIM! JEDEDIAH TOOK...

OH, SORRY! I...

NEVER MIND, ASHLEY! TELL ME WHAT THE HELL'S GOING ON?

JEDEDIAH STOLE THE HELICOPTER AND WENT TO POINT X ALONE!

FOR THE LAST TIME, MR JEDEDIAH, I ORDER YOU TO TURN AROUND! WHAT YOU'RE DOING IS MUTINY! IT'S AN EXTREMELY SERIOUS ACTION DURING A SPACE MISSION!

THE STORM'S ABATED, BUT THE RAIN IS STILL COMING DOWN HARD AND THERE ARE STRONG GUSTS OF WIND. YOU'RE GOING TO COST US OUR PRECIOUS HELICOPTER!

JEDEDIAH THORNTON! YOU'RE PUTTING THE ENTIRE MISSION IN JEOPARDY!

NO! YOU'RE THE ONES WHO COULD RUIN EVERYTHING WITH YOUR ILLOGICAL BEHAVIOUR! I KNEW IT: A MISSION LED BY WOMEN WAS BOUND TO GET HOPELESSLY TWISTED!

I'M GOING TO POINT X TO WAIT FOR THE EXTRATERRESTRIALS IN A DIGNIFIED MANNER! I WILL WELCOME THEM WITH TRUST AND DECENCY AS THE REPRE-SENTATIVE OF THE PEOPLE OF EARTH!

I AM NOT GOING TO WELCOME THEM WHILE BOGGED DOWN BY RIDICULOUS SAFETY MEASURES – AND, MORE IMPORTANTLY, I AM NOT GOING TO WELCOME THEM SURROUNDED BY A GAGGLE OF IMMODEST WOMEN UNWORTHY OF SUCH AN IMPORTANT EVENT FOR MANKIND!

22

SO STOP YOUR POINTLESS YELLING! I AM NOT TURNING AROUND!

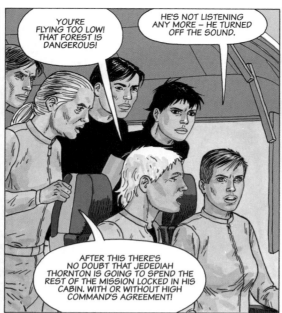

YOU'RE FLYING TOO LOW! THAT FOREST IS DANGEROUS!

HE'S NOT LISTENING ANY MORE – HE TURNED OFF THE SOUND.

AFTER THIS THERE'S NO DOUBT THAT JEDEDIAH THORNTON IS GOING TO SPEND THE REST OF THE MISSION LOCKED IN HIS CABIN. WITH OR WITHOUT HIGH COMMAND'S AGREEMENT!

AND I'M STARTING TO BITTERLY REGRET INFORMING THE AUTHORITIES OF YOUR PUNCHING HIM, KIM KELLER...

LOOK!

THE VIDEO IS GONE! NO... THE INTERNAL FEED IS BACK!

MR JEDEDIAH, ARE YOU INJURED? IS THE HELICOPTER'S COCKPIT INTACT?

23

NO, I'M NOT HURT... NOTHING SERIOUS, ANYWAY... THE COCKPIT... THE COCKPIT SEEMS INTACT, YES.

WHERE'S THE HELICOPTER? WHAT'S AROUND YOU?

I'M INSIDE SOME SORT OF CAVE ... WITH VEGETAL WALLS... IT'S DARK... I DON'T REALLY UNDERSTAND WHERE I AM... THE HELICOPTER'S HALF IMMERGED IN A POOL BUT THE COCKPIT IS STILL SEALED.

IS THE ENGINE STILL WORKING?

NO, AND I CAN'T SEEM TO RESTART IT...

ALL RIGHT. YOU'RE GOING TO STAY INSIDE THE COCKPIT. DON'T TRY TO GET OUT. WE'RE COMING TO GET YOU.

OOPS! SORRY, IT WASN'T MY PLACE TO ASK THOSE QUESTIONS OR DECIDE WHAT WE'D DO – I GOT CARRIED AWAY...

DON'T WORRY ABOUT IT. YOU DID WHAT NEEDED TO BE DONE...

BUT HOW DO YOU INTEND TO GO AND GET HIM? WE HAVE NO OTHER VEHICLE, AND GOING ON FOOT WOULD BE ALMOST IMPOSSIBLE.

THE HOIST. WE HAVE TO USE THE HOIST. BESIDES, WE'LL NEED IT TO RECOVER THE HELICOPTER AND DISENTANGLE IT FROM THE FOREST.

I VOLUNTEER TO GO. ALEXA, WILL YOU COME TOO?

NO! NOT YOU, KIM... ER... I'D RATHER ALEXA AND ZAO WENT.

YES, I AGREE WITH HER, KIM.

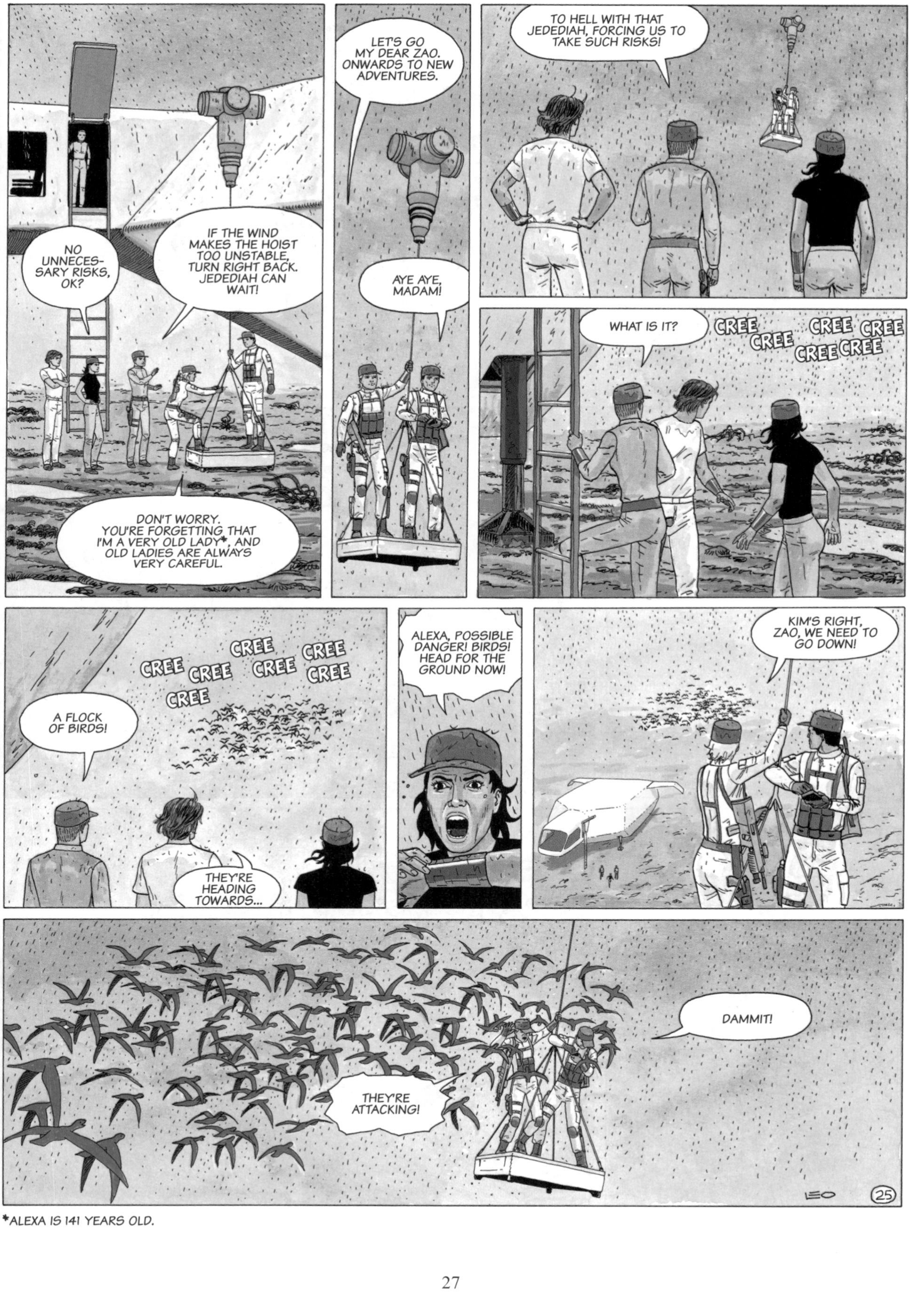
NO UNNECES-SARY RISKS, OK?
IF THE WIND MAKES THE HOIST TOO UNSTABLE, TURN RIGHT BACK. JEDEDIAH CAN WAIT!
DON'T WORRY. YOU'RE FORGETTING THAT I'M A VERY OLD LADY*, AND OLD LADIES ARE ALWAYS VERY CAREFUL.
LET'S GO MY DEAR ZAO. ONWARDS TO NEW ADVENTURES.
AYE AYE, MADAM!
TO HELL WITH THAT JEDEDIAH, FORCING US TO TAKE SUCH RISKS!
WHAT IS IT?
CREE CREE CREE CREE CREE CREE
A FLOCK OF BIRDS!
CREE CREE CREE CREE CREE CREE CREE
THEY'RE HEADING TOWARDS...
ALEXA, POSSIBLE DANGER! BIRDS! HEAD FOR THE GROUND NOW!
KIM'S RIGHT, ZAO, WE NEED TO GO DOWN!
DAMMIT!
THEY'RE ATTACKING!
LEO
25

*ALEXA IS 141 YEARS OLD.

ZAO!

THE BIRDS ARE LEAVING!

HOW IS HE? THAT WAS A LONG WAY DOWN!

HE'S BLEEDING FROM THE NOSE AND EAR – I DON'T LIKE THIS!

HERE COMES DR BLUM!

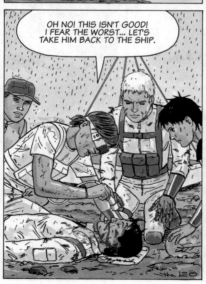

OH NO! THIS ISN'T GOOD! I FEAR THE WORST... LET'S TAKE HIM BACK TO THE SHIP.

THE FOAM WILL SOLIDIFY AND KEEP HIM IMMOBILE.

WHAT ABOUT YOU, ALEXA? ANY DEEP WOUNDS? ARE YOUR EYES ALL RIGHT?

YES, MY EYES ARE FINE AND I DON'T HAVE ANY SERIOUS INJURIES. I JUST HAVE A MILLION SMALL CUTS! DAMN THOSE BIRDS – THEY WERE LIKE FLYING PIRANHAS!

26

IT'S DIFFICULT TO DEFEND AGAINST SUCH SWARMING ATTACKS!

WE HAVE FLAME-THROWERS IN THE ARMOURY. WE'LL HAVE TO MAKE SURE THERE'S ALWAYS SOMEONE WITH A FLAME-THROWER ON FIELD EXPEDITIONS.

'ZAO'S INJURIES WERE SERIOUS: A FRACTURED SKULL AND A CRACKED VERTEBRA. THEY REQUIRED THE SORT OF SURGICAL TREATMENT WE OBVIOUSLY COULDN'T PROVIDE ON SITE. AMOS PUT HIM IN CRYOGENIC STASIS UNTIL WE RETURNED TO BASE CAMP.'

WE LOST AN IMPORTANT ELEMENT. ZAO IS SOMEONE YOU CAN COUNT ON WHEN THINGS GET ROUGH...

WE'RE MORE RESISTANT TO INJURIES, KIM. WE SHOULD BE THE ONES GOING TO GET THE HELICOPTER. GIVE THE DOC A MINUTE TO FINISH BANDAGING ME AND I'LL BE READY TO GO!

NO CAN DO, ALEXA...

YOUR HANDS ARE IN BAD SHAPE. EVEN WITH YOUR ACCELERATED HEALING, YOU STILL NEED SOME TIME TO RECUPERATE. FOR THE NEXT FEW HOURS, YOU'LL BE UNABLE TO HANDLE A WEAPON EFFECTIVELY.

YOU'RE NOT SUPERWOMAN YET, SWEETIE! I'LL GO WITH ASHLEY.

YOU BOTH COME BACK IN ONE PIECE, D'YOU HEAR?

GOOD LUCK!

OH, THAT JEDEDIAH! I WONDER IF WE WOULDN'T BE BETTER OFF LEAVING HIM TO ROT WHERE HE IS INSTEAD OF TAKING ALL THESE RISKS!

WE'RE GOING TO GET THE HELICOPTER BACK, ASHLEY. WE NEED THAT AIRCRAFT – OTHERWISE I WOULDN'T BE GOING. I CAME HERE TO FIND MY DAUGHTER. I CAN'T AFFORD TO RISK MY LIFE FOR NOTHING.

NO, I DON'T BELIEVE THAT. YOU'RE FURIOUS RIGHT NOW, BUT THE TRUTH IS THAT YOU'D BE INCAPABLE OF ABANDONING SOMEONE LIKE THAT. NOT EVEN THAT INSUFFERABLE JEDEDIAH.

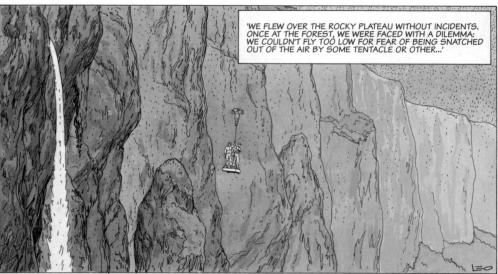

'WE FLEW OVER THE ROCKY PLATEAU WITHOUT INCIDENTS. ONCE AT THE FOREST, WE WERE FACED WITH A DILEMMA: WE COULDN'T FLY TOO LOW FOR FEAR OF BEING SNATCHED OUT OF THE AIR BY SOME TENTACLE OR OTHER...'

'...NOR DID WE WANT TO FLY TOO HIGH, TO AVOID ATTRACTING MORE OF THE BLASTED PIRANHA-BIRDS!'

CAN'T YOU MAKE THIS THING GO FASTER, ASHLEY?

I'M ALREADY AT THE LIMIT, KIM! ANY MORE AND I'D LOSE CONTROL OF THIS PIECE OF CRAP!

AND THE RAIN'S PICKING UP. DAMMIT!

WHAT THE HELL?! THE RAIN'S BECOMING LIKE JELLY!

ANIMALS! MILLIONS OF TINY ANIMALS TRAVELLING IN RAINDROPS! INCREDIBLE!

ANIMALS?! URGH! THAT'S DISGUSTING!

ASHLEY!...

28

30

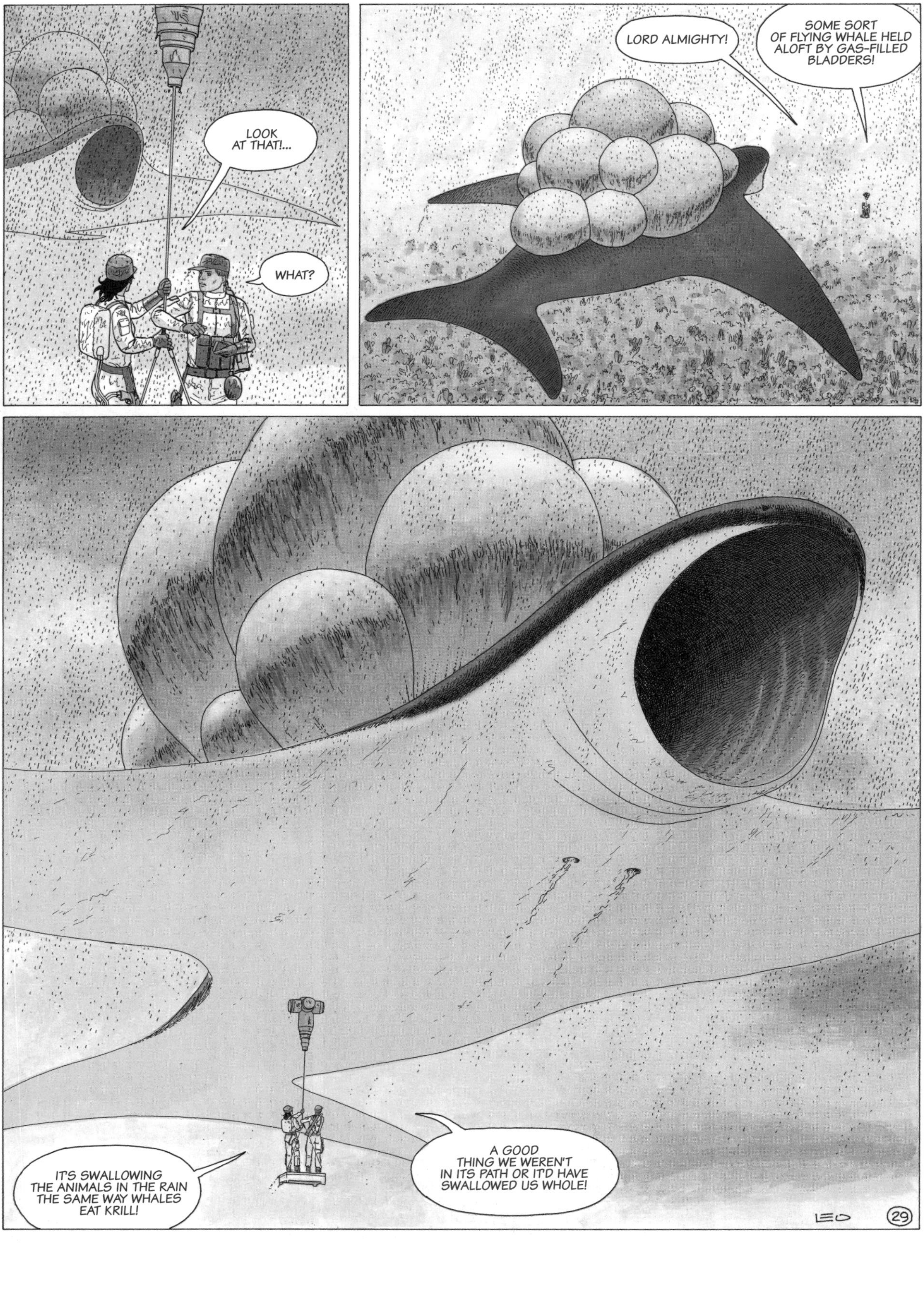
LOOK AT THAT!...
WHAT?
LORD ALMIGHTY!
SOME SORT OF FLYING WHALE HELD ALOFT BY GAS-FILLED BLADDERS!
IT'S SWALLOWING THE ANIMALS IN THE RAIN THE SAME WAY WHALES EAT KRILL!
A GOOD THING WE WEREN'T IN ITS PATH OR IT'D HAVE SWALLOWED US WHOLE!
LEO
29

OR IT WOULD'VE AVOIDED US LIKE WHALES DO...

WE'RE GETTING CLOSE. OVER THERE – SEE THAT BROKEN BRANCH?

WHAT DO WE DO? THE THING THAT CAUGHT THE HELICOPTER COULD GO AFTER US TOO...

YES. BRING THE HOIST DOWN INTO THE FOREST HERE. WE'LL MAKE A LATERAL APPROACH.

GO AHEAD, ASHLEY. WE HAVE TO SNAKE OUR WAY THROUGH THE PLANTS. THE CHOPPER IS STRAIGHT AHEAD.

YOU OK?

I'M SCARED OUT OF MY MIND, KIM! THIS PLACE IS TERRIFYING!

WHERE'S THAT DAMNED HELICOPTER? IT SHOULD BE HERE!

KEEP GOING, SLOWLY...

30

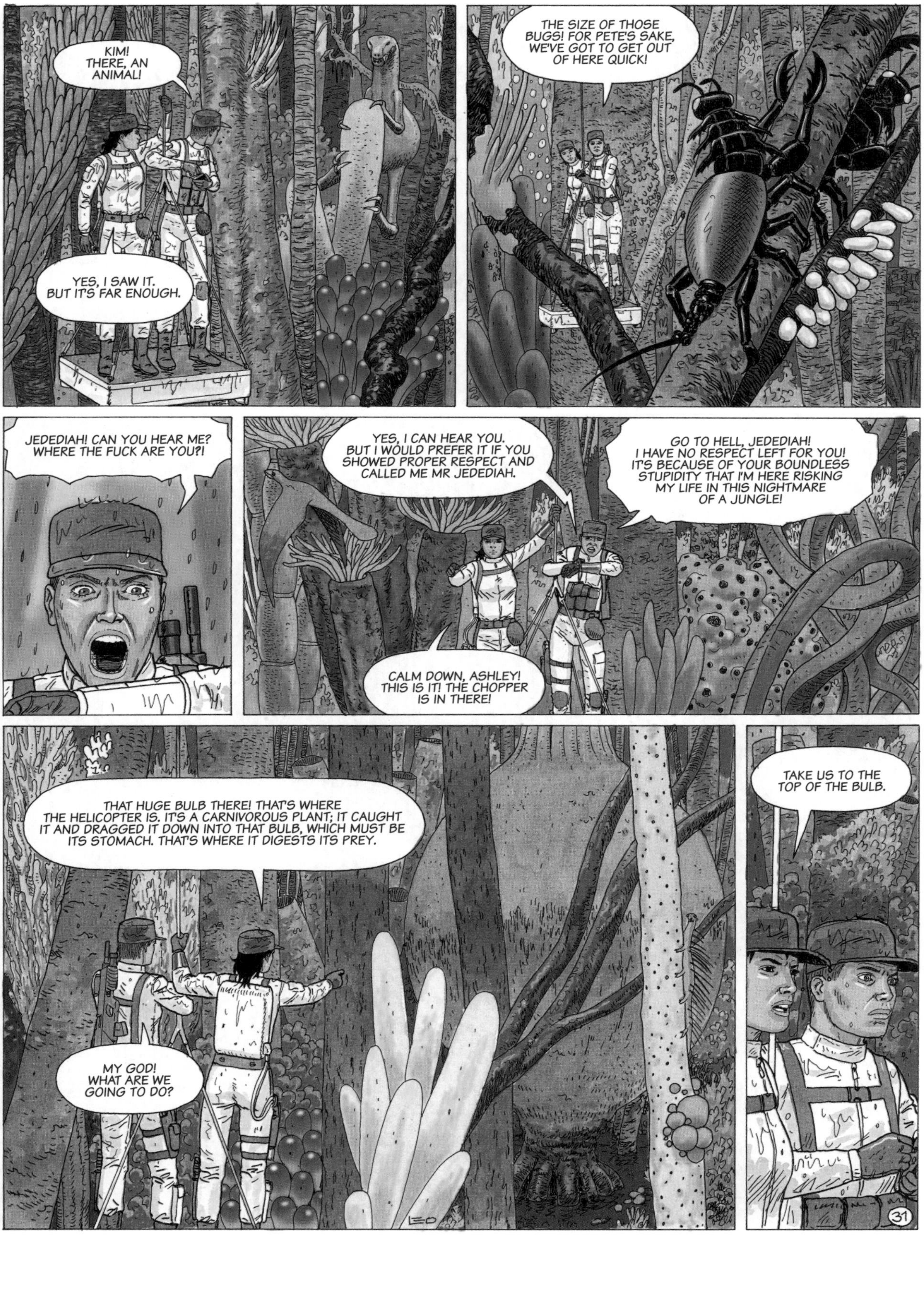
KIM! THERE, AN ANIMAL!
YES, I SAW IT. BUT IT'S FAR ENOUGH.
THE SIZE OF THOSE BUGS! FOR PETE'S SAKE, WE'VE GOT TO GET OUT OF HERE QUICK!
JEDEDIAH! CAN YOU HEAR ME? WHERE THE FUCK ARE YOU?!
YES, I CAN HEAR YOU. BUT I WOULD PREFER IT IF YOU SHOWED PROPER RESPECT AND CALLED ME MR JEDEDIAH.
GO TO HELL, JEDEDIAH! I HAVE NO RESPECT LEFT FOR YOU! IT'S BECAUSE OF YOUR BOUNDLESS STUPIDITY THAT I'M HERE RISKING MY LIFE IN THIS NIGHTMARE OF A JUNGLE!
CALM DOWN, ASHLEY! THIS IS IT! THE CHOPPER IS IN THERE!
THAT HUGE BULB THERE! THAT'S WHERE THE HELICOPTER IS. IT'S A CARNIVOROUS PLANT; IT CAUGHT IT AND DRAGGED IT DOWN INTO THAT BULB, WHICH MUST BE ITS STOMACH. THAT'S WHERE IT DIGESTS ITS PREY.
MY GOD! WHAT ARE WE GOING TO DO?
LEO
TAKE US TO THE TOP OF THE BULB.
31

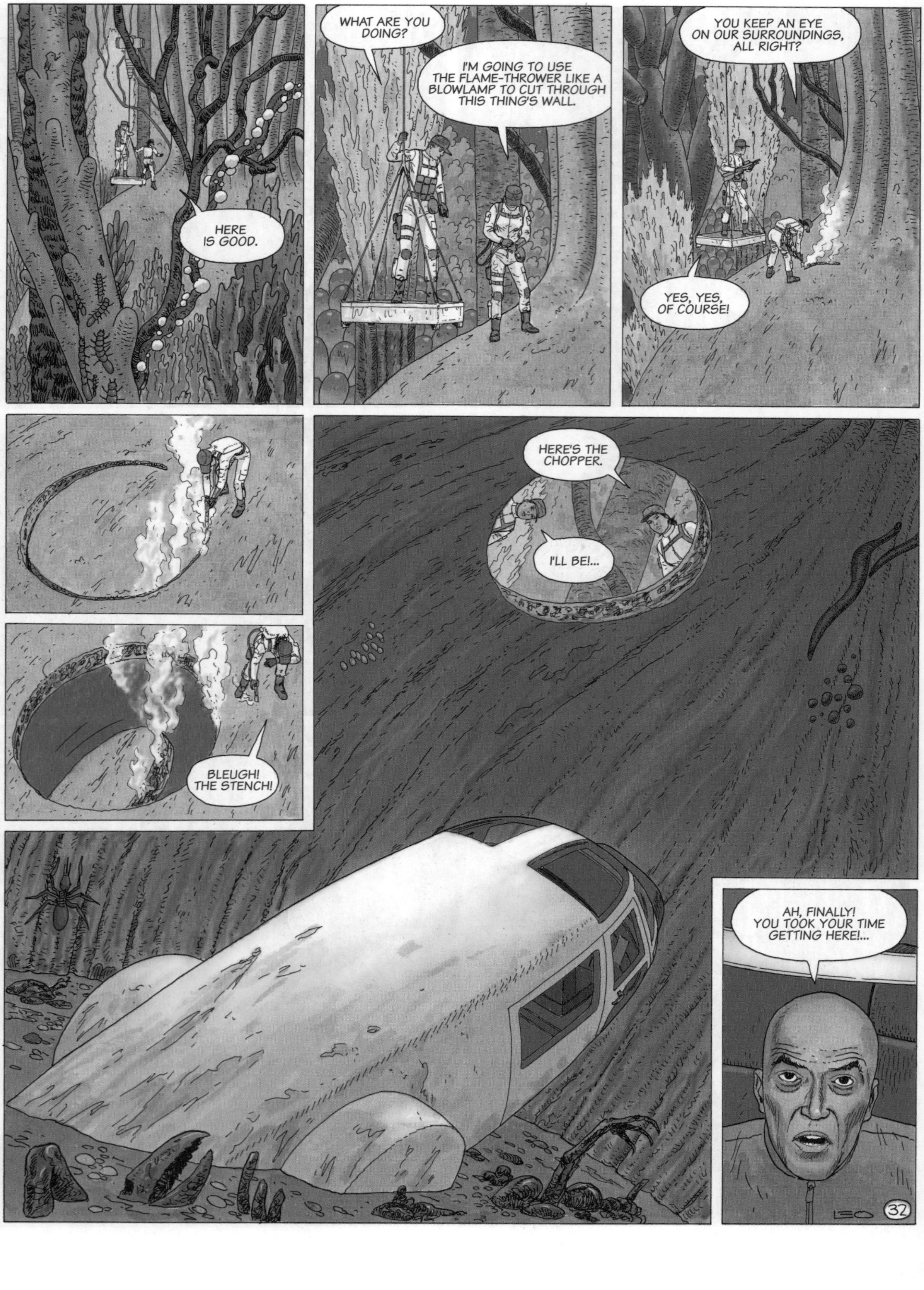
HERE IS GOOD.
WHAT ARE YOU DOING?
I'M GOING TO USE THE FLAME-THROWER LIKE A BLOWLAMP TO CUT THROUGH THIS THING'S WALL.
YOU KEEP AN EYE ON OUR SURROUNDINGS, ALL RIGHT?
YES, YES, OF COURSE!
BLEUGH! THE STENCH!
HERE'S THE CHOPPER.
I'LL BE!...
AH, FINALLY! YOU TOOK YOUR TIME GETTING HERE!...
LEO
32

HA HA HA HA HA HA HA H

JEDEDIAH THORNTON, YOUR ARE THE MOST UNPLEASANT, ANNOYING, WRETCHED PERSON I'VE EVER MET!

STOP INSULTING ME, WOMAN!

NASTY PLACE!

OH NO! BAD NEWS...

WE CAN WRITE OFF THE HELICOPTER! THE TAIL BROKE OFF.

DAMMIT!

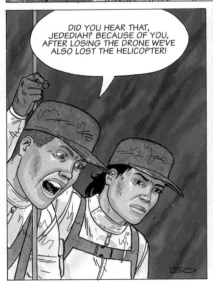

DID YOU HEAR THAT, JEDEDIAH? BECAUSE OF YOU, AFTER LOSING THE DRONE WE'VE ALSO LOST THE HELICOPTER!

AND MR ZAO WAS SERIOUSLY INJURED TRYING TO COME AND RESCUE YOU TOO! YOU ARE ABSOLUTELY DESPICABLE, JEDEDIAH THORNTON!

I DEMAND YOU TREAT ME WITH RESPECT, WOMAN!

33

ALL RIGHT, LET'S CUT OUT THE YELLING AND GO HOME. COME ON, JEDEDIAH.

NO, THIS PLATFORM IS TOO SMALL. IT WOULD FORCE ME TO PRESS AGAINST YOU – TWO WOMEN IN CLOSE-FITTING UNIFORMS. THAT'S OUT OF THE QUESTION! YOU MAY EVEN BE WEARING NOTHING UNDERNEATH!

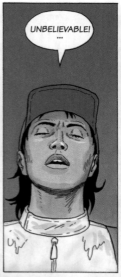

UNBELIEVABLE! ...

THIS GUY'S INSANE!

NO, I'M NOT INSANE. I'M SIMPLY VIRTUOUS – A CONCEPT THAT MUST BE ENTIRELY ALIEN TO YOU, OBVIOUSLY. I WILL LEAVE ALONE ON THIS CONTRAPTION, AND YOU WILL WAIT HERE UNTIL SOMEONE COMES TO GET YOU.

WHAT ARE YOU...?!

BZZZT

KIM KELLER! WHAT DID YOU DO TO MR JEDEDIAH?!

I STUNNED HIM WITH A LITTLE ELECTRIC JOLT, MADAM. HE'LL BE FINE... THOUGH HE'LL HAVE A SPLITTING HEADACHE...

ARE YOU SURE YOU HAD YOUR STUN BATON PROPERLY SET, KIM? HE'S JUST LYING THERE LIFELESS!

TO BE PERFECTLY HONEST, ASHLEY, I'M NOT REALLY SURE. IT'S THE FIRST TIME I'VE USED THIS THING – AND I WAS VERY CROSS...

JUST THEN, AT BASE CAMP...

WHAT IS IT?

WE'RE HERE TO SEE YOUR DAUGHTER, LORNA WHITE. I'M TRANSFERRING TO YOUR WRIST-COM THE JUDGE ORDER AUTHORISING US TO DO SO.

WHAT'S THE MEANING OF THIS?!

HMM... FINE, I'LL CALL HER.

NONE OF THAT, MR WHITE. YOU ARE NOT GOING TO SLAM THE DOOR IN OUR FACE!

YOU HAVE NO RIGHT TO INVADE OUR HOME! GET OUT!

LORNA! THIS IS THE POLICE! WE WANT TO TALK TO YOU – SEE IF YOU'RE ALL RIGHT!

WE HAVE THE RIGHT TO USE ANY MEANS AT OUR DISPOSAL TO SPEAK TO LORNA WHITE. THAT'S IN THE JUDGE ORDER.

HELP!

SHE BROUGHT IT ON HERSELF! SHE'S A REBEL – WE HAD TO BREAK HER!

DON'T MOVE, SIR!

DON'T LET HIM HIT ME AGAIN! PLEASE DON'T LET HIM HIT ME!

LORNA!

MY GOD!

IT'S TAKING THEM A LONG TIME TO COME OUT... IS THAT A GOOD SIGN?

I DON'T KNOW... MAYBE...

AN AMBULANCE! OH, NO!...

LEO

35

I SUGGEST WE DON'T DISCUSS JEDEDIAH THORNTON'S CASE DURING OUR MEAL. IT MIGHT DISRUPT OUR DIGESTION. ISN'T THAT RIGHT, DR BLUM?

ABSOLUTELY, MADAM!

TELL ME, OUR MYSTERIOUS SPHERE HAS BEEN FLOATING OVER ITS LITTLE CRATER FOR A WHILE NOW, NOT MOVING AN INCH. WHAT ARE WE GOING TO DO? WAIT INDEFINITELY? SET A DEADLINE?

IT'S HARD TO ANSWER THAT, SURIA. WE DON'T...

BEEP BEEP BEEP BEEP

THE PROXIMITY ALERT!

THAT'S YOUR QUESTION ANSWERED, SURIA...

THE SPHERE CAME TO US!

IT APPEARED INSTANTANEOUSLY! IF YOU REWIND THE RECORDING IN SLOW MOTION, THERE'S NOTHING, THEN SUDDENLY IT'S THERE. IT'S INCREDIBLE!

BEEP BEEP BEEP BEEP BEEP BEE

WHAT IS IT THIS TIME?

THE RADAR!

DID THE SPHERE...?

NO, IT'S SOMETHING ELSE... OH MY GOD!... ALEXA, ARE YOU SEEING WHAT I'M SEEING?...

WELL?

A SPACESHIP A LITTLE SMALLER THAN OUR SHUTTLE CAME DOWN FROM SPACE AND LANDED THREE MILES FROM HERE...

36

AN ALIEN SPACESHIP!
WHAT SHOULD WE DO?
LOOK!
THE SPHERE IS CHANGING!
ARE WE IN DANGER? I MEAN, SHOULD WE PREP THE SHUTTLE FOR AN EMERGENCY DEPARTURE?
IT'S GONE!
IF IT MAKES YOU FEEL ANY BETTER... BUT WE CAME HERE TO MEET THE ALIENS POTENTIALLY PRESENT ON THIS PLANET. SINCE THEY SEEM TO BE SHOWING UP AT LAST, NOW'S NOT THE TIME TO THINK ABOUT LEAVING.
FIVE MILES AWAY...
THE SPHERE IS STARTING TO REACT. IT COULD GET DANGEROUS...
ON THE CONTRARY! IT'S A GOOD SIGN. THE WORST THING WOULD BE NO REACTION – WE COULD END UP WAITING FOR EVER.
BUT IT'S STILL DANGEROUS. THESE HUMANS ARE SUCH DISORDERLY PEOPLE!
YOU'RE EXAGGERATING! THEY'RE ALSO DARING AND INVENTIVE. I LIKE THAT.
OF COURSE YOU LIKE THAT! SPEAKING OF WHICH, HOW DOES IT FEEL, SEEING THAT HUMAN FEMALE AGAIN?
I STILL FIND HER INTENSELY FASCINATING ... AND I FEEL TERRIBLY GUILTY!
LEO
37

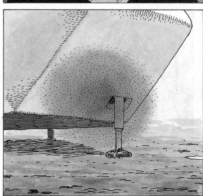

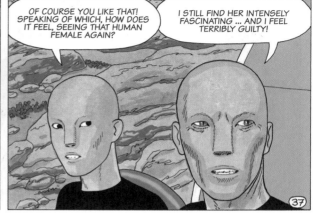

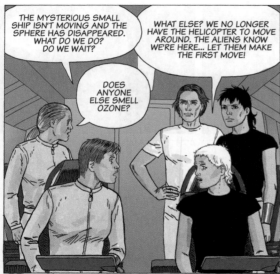

THE MYSTERIOUS SMALL SHIP ISN'T MOVING AND THE SPHERE HAS DISAPPEARED. WHAT DO WE DO? DO WE WAIT?

WHAT ELSE? WE NO LONGER HAVE THE HELICOPTER TO MOVE AROUND. THE ALIENS KNOW WE'RE HERE... LET THEM MAKE THE FIRST MOVE!

DOES ANYONE ELSE SMELL OZONE?

HEY! THERE!

HOW DID THAT THING GET IN?! THE DOORS ARE CLOSED – THE SHUTTLE IS SEALED!

I'VE DEALT WITH A SIMILAR SPHERE ONCE... IT WAS A CAMERA.

BE CAREFUL, KIM!

I CAN'T MOVE IT! IT'S AS IF IT WAS NAILED TO AN INVISIBLE BASE.

IT'S STICKY! JUST LIKE THE LARGE SPHERE! THIS ONE ISN'T A CAMERA, THAT'S FOR SURE!

IT'S MOVING!

'SLOWLY, WITHOUT A SOUND, THE SMALL SPHERE BEGAN FLYING AROUND THE COCKPIT AS IF IT WAS EXAMINING US. NO ONE DARED TO BREATHE!'

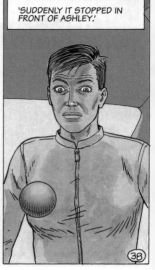

'SUDDENLY IT STOPPED IN FRONT OF ASHLEY.'

38

40

'THEN IT MOVED TOWARDS HER CHEST...'

HEY!

'...AND TO OUR ASTONISHMENT AND HORROR, IT ENTERED ASHLEY'S BODY AS IF IT HAD BEEN AN IMMATERIAL HOLOGRAM RATHER THAN THE SOLID SPHERE I HAD TOUCHED MERE MOMENTS BEFORE.'

AH!

WHAT ON WEARTH...?!...

NOTHING'S GOING TO HAPPEN TO YOU, ASHLEY! I PROMISE! HOLD ME, HOLD ME TIGHT – I'M WITH YOU, AND I'M SURE THAT THING MEANS US ABSOLUTELY NO HARM.

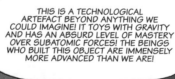

IT'S COMING OUT! IT'S OVER, ASHLEY!

THERE, THAT'S IT! THE SPHERE CAME OUT AND IT DIDN'T HURT YOU!

IT'S BECOME SOLID AGAIN, AND COMPLETELY IMPERVIOUS TO ANY PRESSURE I CAN EXERT. IT'S INCREDIBLE!

IT MUST BE SOME SORT OF PROBE. IT CAME TO ANALYSE US, SEE WHO WE ARE, WHAT WE'RE MADE OF.

THIS IS A TECHNOLOGICAL ARTEFACT BEYOND ANYTHING WE COULD IMAGINE! IT TOYS WITH GRAVITY AND HAS AN ABSURD LEVEL OF MASTERY OVER SUBATOMIC FORCES! THE BEINGS WHO BUILT THIS OBJECT ARE IMMENSELY MORE ADVANCED THAN WE ARE!

IT'S LEAVING!

AND THAT'S HOW IT CAME IN – SIMPLY BY GOING THROUGH THE WALL!

39

COME WITH ME, ASHLEY. I'M GOING TO GIVE YOU A PILL, THEN YOU CAN LIE DOWN IN YOUR CABIN FOR A LITTLE WHILE.

YOU SHOULDN'T BE AFRAID OF WHAT HAPPENED TO YOU, ASHLEY SCOTT. THE BEINGS BEHIND THAT SPHERE CAN'T POSSIBLY BE MALICIOUS. I'M SURE THEY WOULD NEVER DO ANYTHING THAT COULD BRING US HARM!

'SURIA SEEMED MORE SINCERE THAN ME WHEN SHE SAID THAT. IF I'D BEEN ASHLEY, I'D HAVE CLUNG TO THE HOPE THAT WHAT WE WERE TELLING HER WAS TRUE.'

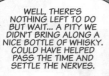

WELL, THERE'S NOTHING LEFT TO DO BUT WAIT... A PITY WE DIDN'T BRING ALONG A NICE BOTTLE OF WHISKY. COULD HAVE HELPED PASS THE TIME AND SETTLE THE NERVES.

MEANWHILE...

NO, YOU'RE NOT UGLY. YOU'RE A PRETTY GIRL WHO GOT ATTACKED. THAT'S NOT THE SAME.

HOSPITAL

GATE B

THE MAIN THING IS THAT YOU'RE NOT IN PAIN. IT'S NOT HURTING, IS IT?

NO. THAT STUFF THEY GAVE ME IS MAGICAL: ALL THE PAIN JUST VANISHED!

HELLO? CAN I COME IN?

I BRING YOU A VISITOR, LORNA. A SURPRISE VISITOR.

POLICE

POLICE

POLI

LANA!

OH, SWEETIE! WHAT DID THEY DO TO YOU?

THEY LET YOU COME AND SEE ME?!

THEY HAD LITTLE CHOICE. THE JUDGE MADE IT ILLEGAL TO FORCE MINORS TO WEAR THOSE HUMILIATING INFLATABLE CLOTHES AND BE CONFINED AT HOME.

WHAT ABOUT MY PARENTS? WHAT HAPPENED TO THEM?

THEY WERE ARRESTED, ALONG WITH MINE. THEY'VE BEEN CHARGED WITH CHILD ABUSE. YOUR FATHER GOT THE WORST OF IT: ASSAULT, ACTS OF TORTURE, MORAL HARASSMENT...

LET'S LEAVE THESE GIRLS ALONE. THEY'VE EARNED IT.

CONGRATULATIONS ON THE POLICE'S RESPONSE TIME! IF IT HADN'T BEEN FOR YOU, LORNA COULD HAVE DIED. HER FATHER GAVE HER SUCH A VIOLENT BLOW TO THE STOMACH THAT IT CAUSED INTERNAL BLEEDING. SHE HAD TO HAVE EMERGENCY SURGERY!

WHAT A FOUL INDIVIDUAL! BUT HE'S GOING TO SPEND A GOOD LONG WHILE IN PRISON THIS TIME!

THERE'S GOING TO BE A SLIGHT PROBLEM WHEN LORNA LEAVES THE HOSPITAL: SHE WON'T BE ALLOWED TO LIVE ALONE AT HER PARENTS...

BUT... SHE'S STAYING WITH ME – WE'LL KEEP LIVING TOGETHER.

WITH YOU TWO? IN A SINGLE ROOM? NO, THE JUDGE WON'T AGREE TO THAT.

WHAT DO YOU MEAN? MAI LAN AND I AREN'T LIVING TOGETHER!

OH? I THOUGHT...

MARK IS KIM KELLER'S PARTNER...

KIM KELLER'S? OH, OK, I GOT IT ALL MIXED UP. NO PROBLEM, THEN. LORNA ALREADY HAS A HOME. THAT'S GOOD!

I WONDER HOW THINGS ARE GOING FOR KIM. IT'S HARD NOT BEING ABLE TO COMMUNICATE WITH HER, ISN'T IT?

YES... THE BEST THING TO DO IS NOT TO THINK ABOUT IT, MAI LAN.

SO THAT POLICE OFFICER THOUGHT THE TWO OF US LIVED TOGETHER. HOW ABOUT THAT!...

SHE MUST HAVE SEEN US TOGETHER OFTEN AND...

TELL ME...

YES?

DO YOU THINK KIM HAS FEELINGS FOR THAT DOCTOR, AMOS BLUM? BECAUSE HE'S CERTAINLY NOT SHY ABOUT PURSUING HER!

ER... I DON'T KNOW, MARK. I REALLY DON'T KNOW...

OK... I'LL LEAVE YOU TO IT, THEN. CALL ME?

YES...

UNIT B3

42

'TWO HOURS AFTER THE SMALL SPHERE'S APPEARANCE INSIDE THE SHUTTLE, NOTHING HAD HAPPENED...'

I STOPPED BY TO SEE HOW JEDEDIAH IS DOING. HE'S FURIOUS, HYSTERICAL, AND THREATENS TO SET FIRE TO HIS CABIN UNLESS WE LET HIM OUT.

CAN'T YOU SEDATE HIM, AMOS? PLEASE, MAKE HIM SLEEP UNTIL WE GO BACK!

UNFORTUNATELY, I CAN'T DO THAT, KIM. IT'S NOT ETHICAL FOR A DOCTOR.

BUT I...

KIM! LOOK! OUTSIDE!

LYNN!

LYNN'S ALIVE!

YOU WERE RIGHT, KIM! YOU WERE RIGHT!

LYNN! SWEETHEART! MUMMY'S HERE!

LYNN!

AH!

NO!

43

WHY DO THIS TO ME?! WHY? IT'S NOT FAIR! IT'S JUST NOT FAIR!

THAT... THAT'S ABSURD!

WE MUST GO AND TALK TO THEM! I CAN'T WATCH KIM GOING THROUGH SUCH TRAUMA AND DO NOTHING! WE KNOW THINGS THEY DON'T KNOW YET — WE CAN HELP THEM!

NO!

WE WILL MAKE CONTACT ONLY AFTER THE LITTLE GIRL APPEARS — IF SHE APPEARS. THOSE ARE OUR ORDERS!

HOLOGRAPHIC PICTURES! HOW CAN ANYONE DO SOMETHING SO MEAN?! DO YOU HAVE AN EXPLANATION, ALEXA?

NONE, DOC! IT'S COMPLETELY INSANE! WHOEVER'S BEHIND THAT DAMNED SPHERE IS HAVING FUN TORTURING US!

I DON'T THINK THERE'S ANYONE BEHIND THAT SPHERE. I THINK IT'S JUST A MACHINE. HYPER-SOPHISTICATED, YES, BUT NONETHELESS JUST A MACHINE...

THE IMAGES ARE FADING...

THE YOUNG WOMAN MUST BE ZAO'S SISTER*...

I THINK THE APPEARANCE OF THE HOLOGRAMS IS A VERY GOOD SIGN, KIM KELLER. THE SPHERE IS BEGINNING TO UNDERSTAND WHO WE ARE... I'M CERTAIN IT'S ALMOST READY TO RETURN YOUR DAUGHTER TO YOU!

FEELING BETTER? DO YOU WANT TO LIE DOWN IN YOUR CABIN FOR A WHILE?

NO, I'M FINE...

YOU'RE GOING TO GET YOUR DAUGHTER BACK, KIM! STAY STRONG!

*SEE VOLUME 1

TWEE TWEE TWEE TWEE TWEE

WHAT IS IT?

THE PROXIMITY ALERT! THE SENSORS HAVE DETECTED SOMETHING!

OH MY GOD! NEXT TO US!

A SHUTTLE IDENTICAL TO OURS! THE SPHERE CREATED A SHUTTLE IDENTICAL TO OURS!

COULD IT BE A HOLOGRAM TOO?

LET'S GO AND SEE!

BAM BAM

LET ME OUT THIS INSTANT OR I'LL START A FIRE!

IT MIGHT BE BETTER TO RELEASE HIM, DON'T YOU THINK? HE'S ACTUALLY CAPABLE OF DOING WHAT HE SAYS!

YES, I'LL LET HIM OUT. YOU'RE OK WITH THAT, KIM?

I DON'T CARE! DO WHAT YOU WANT!

45

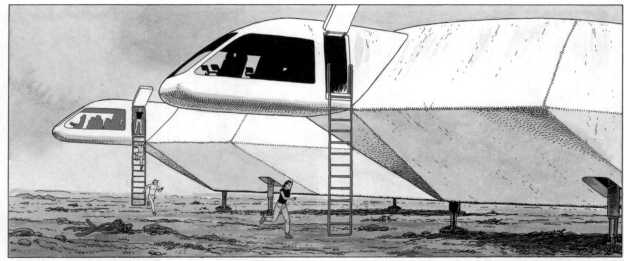

IS IT SOLID?

YES, IT'S NOT A HOLOGRAPHIC PROJECTION!

THIS IS BEYOND COMPREHENSION! THAT SPHERE CAN DO ANYTHING!

THE QUESTION IS WHY? WHY DID THE SPHERE DEEM IT NECESSARY TO MAKE AN EXACT COPY OF OUR SHUTTLE?

IT'S A SPACESHIP... MAYBE THE BEINGS WHO ARE BEHIND THE SPHERE WANT US TO GET ON BOARD, SO THEY CAN TAKE US SOMEWHERE...

THAT'S THE ONLY EXPLANATION, YES! WE'RE FINALLY ABOUT TO MEET THE EXTRATERRESTRIALS.

END OF VOLUME 5

LEO 2013

46